CLASSIC
FILM
SCRIPTS

POTEMKIN

a film by

Sergei Eisenstein

translated from the Russian
by Gillon R. Aitken

Simon and Schuster, New York

General Editor: Sandra Wake

Library of Congress Catalog Card Number: 68-26000

This edition is for sale only in the United States of America,
its territories, possessions, protectorates and places mandated to it,
the Philippines and the Dominion of Canada

Manufactured in Great Britain by Villiers Publications Ltd,
London NW5

CONTENTS

ACKNOWLEDGEMENTS

We wish to thank Lawrence & Wishart Ltd, for granting permission to reproduce the essay contained in their book *Eisenstein, Notes of A Film Director,* translated from the Russian by X. Danko.

Our thanks are also due to l'Avant-Scène du Cinéma and the British Film Institute for the use of their stills.

HISTORY

In the failed Revolution of 1905 against the Russian Tsar, a mutiny took place on board the battleship Potemkin. It was the ship with the best guns and discipline in the Imperial Russian fleet. There were revolutionary cells aboard the Potemkin and the other four ships sailing with her in the Black Sea squadron; but spies usually kept the ships' officers informed of possible rebellion. The revolutionaries hoped to seize the fleet and blockade the ports to help the revolution ashore.

Bad food, especially maggotty meat served for weeks on end, had made the sailors listen to the revolutionaries. On July 5th, a deck-hand complained about the meat to the second-in-command, ' a Polish aristocrat and a tyrant ' in the words of an engineer on the Potemkin. The officer shot the deck-hand, then was shot and flung over the side by other members of the crew. A sailor called Matyushenko became the leader of the mutineers, who seized the armoury when the armoury guard refused to fire at them. Five or six of the ship's officers were executed, the captain shot dead, and the rest of the officers flung overboard, still alive.

The battleship Potemkin then sailed to Odessa. A landing party looking for food and coal was seized by the authorities; but it was released when the rebels threatened to fire on the city. Fellow revolutionaries ashore sent out food and coal to the battleship, which sailed away when other ships from the Black Sea fleet failed to follow her example. Soon, quarrels broke out among the mutineers and the battleship was handed over to the Rumanian government, which released the sailors to go their separate ways.

Sergei Eisenstein's version of this revolutionary episode departs from the facts for the purposes of propaganda and art. There was, for instance, no actual massacre on the Odessa steps. Yet the film is the most moving and inspiring tribute to the Russian Revolution ever made.

ANDREW SINCLAIR, 1968

6

INTRODUCTION
by Sergei Eisenstein

When *Potemkin* is discussed two of its features are commonly
noted : the organic unity of its composition as a whole and
the pathos* of the film.

Taking these two most characteristic features of *Potemkin,*
let us analyze by what means they were achieved, primarily in
the field of composition. We shall study the first feature in
the composition of the film as a whole. For the second, we
shall take the episode of the Odessa steps, where the pathos
of the film reaches its climax, and then we shall apply our
conclusions to the whole.

We shall concern ourselves with the compositional means
employed to ensure these qualities. In the same way we could
study other factors; we could examine the contribution to
organic unity and pathos made by the actors' performances,
by the treatment of the story, by the light and colour scale
of the photography, by the natural backgrounds, by the mass
scenes, etc. But here we shall confine ourselves to one particular problem, that of *structure,* and shall not attempt an
exhaustive analysis of all the film's aspects.

And yet, in an organic work of art, elements that nourish
the work as a whole pervade all the features composing this
work. A unified canon pierces not only the whole and each of
its parts, but also each element that is called to participate
in the work of composition. One and the same principle will
feed any element, appearing in each in a qualitatively different
form. Only in this case are we justified in considering a work

---

* The word is used here in its original sense. — *Tr.*

of art organic, the notion ' organism ' being used in the sense in which Engels spoke of it in his *Dialectics of Nature*: ' The organism is certainly a *higher unity* '.

This brings us to the first item of our analysis — the organic unity of the composition of *Potemkin*.

Let us approach this problem from the premise that the organic unity of a work of art and the sensation of unity can be attained only if the law of building the work answers the law of structure in natural organic phenomena, of which Lenin said that ' the particular does not exist outside that relationship which leads to the general. The general exists only in the particular, through the particular '.

The first analysis will provide material for the study of laws governing unity in static conditions; the second will enable us to study the dynamic operation of these laws. Thus, in the first instance we shall deal with parts and *proportions* in the structure of the work. In the second — with the *movement* of the structure of the work.

Outwardly, *Potemkin* is a chronicle of events but it impresses the spectators as a drama.

The secret of this effect lies in the plot which is built up in accordance with the laws of austere composition of tragedy in its traditional five-act form.

The events, first taken as unembellished facts, are divided into five tragic acts, the facts themselves so arranged as to form a consecutive whole, closely conforming to the requirements of classical tragedy: a third act distinct from the second, a fifth distinct from the first, and so on.

This age-honoured structure of tragedy is further stressed by the subtitle each act is preceded by.

Here are the five acts :

I. *Men and Maggots*

Exposition of the action. The conditions aboard the battleship. Meat teeming with maggots. Unrest among the sailors.

II. *Drama on the Quarter-Deck*

'All hands on deck!' The sailors' refusal to eat the soup. The tarpaulin scene. 'Brothers!' Refusal to fire. Mutiny. Revenge on the officers.

III. *The Dead Man Cries for Vengeance*

Mist. Vakulinchuk's body in the Odessa port. Mourning over the body. Meeting. Raising the red flag.

IV. *The Odessa Steps*

Fraternization of shore and battleship. Yawls with provisions. Shooting on the Odessa steps.

V. *Meeting the Squadron*

Night of expectation. Meeting the squadron. Engines. 'Brothers!' The squadron refuses to fire.

The action in each part is different, but the whole action is permeated and cemented, as it were, by the method of double repetition.

In 'Drama on the Quarter-Deck' a handful of mutinous sailors — part of the battleship's crew — cry '*Brothers!*' to the firing squad. The rifles are lowered. The whole of the crew joins the rebels.

In 'Meeting the Squadron' the mutinous ship — part of the navy — throws the cry '*Brothers!*' to the crews of the admiralty squadron. And the guns trained on the *Potemkin* are lowered. The whole of the fleet is at one with the *Potemkin*.

From a particle of the battleship's organism to the organism as a whole; from a particle of the navy's organism — the battleship — to the navy's organism as a whole. This is how the feeling of revolutionary brotherhood develops thematically; and the composition of the work on the subject of the brotherhood of workers and of revolution develops parallel with it.

9

Over the heads of censors, the film spreads in bourgeois countries the idea of the brotherhood of workers, carrying to them the brotherly 'Hurrah! ' — just as in the film itself the idea of revolutionary brotherhood spreads from the rebellious ship to the shore.

As far as emotional impact and idea are concerned, that alone would be enough to make the film an organic whole, but we would like to test its structure from the standpoint of form.

In its five parts, tied with the general thematic line, there is otherwise little that is similar externally. Structurally, though, they are perfectly *identical* in that each act is clearly divided into two almost equal parts, this division becoming more pronounced in part II.

The tarpaulin scene — mutiny.

Mourning for Vakulinchuk — meeting of indignant protest.

Fraternizing — shooting.

Anxiously awaiting the squadron — triumph.

Moreover, every 'transition' point is emphasized by a pause, a *caesura*.

In part III this is a few shots of clenched fists, showing the transition from grief for the slain comrade to infuriated protest.

In part IV this is the title ' *SUDDENLY . . .'*, cutting short the fraternizing scene and ushering in the shooting scene.

In part II this is the motionless rifle muzzles; in part V — the gaping mouths of the guns and the exclamation, ' *Brothers!* ', breaking the dead silence of expectation and arousing an avalanche of fraternal feelings.

And the remarkable thing about these dividing points is that they mark not merely a transition to a merely *different* mood, to a merely *different* rhythm, to a merely *different* event, but show each time that the transition is to a sharply opposite quality. To say that we have contrasts would not be enough : the image of the same theme is each time presented from the *opposite* point of view, although it *grows*

10

out of the theme itself.

Thus, the rebellion breaks out after the unbearable strain of waiting under the rifles (part II).

The angry protest follows the mass mourning for the slain comrade (part III).

The shooting on the Odessa steps is a natural answer of the reactionaries to the fraternal embraces between the mutinous crew of the *Potemkin* and the population of Odessa (part IV).

The unity of such a canon, recurring in each act of the drama, is very significant.

This unity is characteristic of the *structure* of the *Potemkin* as a whole.

The film in its entirety is also divided near the middle by a dead halt, a *caesura,* when the tempestuous action of the first half is suspended, and the second half begins to gain impetus.

The episode with Vakulinchuk's body and the Odessa mist serves as a similar *caesura* for the film as a whole.

At that point the theme of revolution spreads from one mutinous battleship to Odessa, embracing the whole city topographically opposed to the ship but emotionally at one with it. But at the moment when the theme returns to the sea, the city is separated from it by soldiers (the episode on the steps).

We see that the development of the theme is organic and that the structure of the film born of this thematic development *is identical in the whole as it is in its parts, large and small.*

The law of unity has been observed throughout.

In terms of proportions, organic unity is expressed in what is known in aesthetics as ' golden section '.

A work of art built on the principle of the golden section is usually most effective.

This principle has been exhaustively applied in the plastic arts.

It is applied less in such arts as music and poetry, although

11

we may safely say that there is a vast field of application in these.

I don't think that a motion picture has ever been subjected to a test on the golden-section principle.

All the more interesting, therefore, is the fact that *Potemkin,* whose organic unity is well known, has been based on this principle.

In speaking about the division of each part of the film and of the film as a whole, we said ' two *almost* equal parts '. In fact, the proportion is closer to 2:3, which approximates the golden section.

The main *caesura* of the film, the ' *zero* ' point at which action is suspended, is between the end of part II and the beginning of part III — the 2:3 ratio.

To be more exact, it is *at the end of part II,* for it is there that the theme of dead Vakulinchuk is introduced, and the *caesurae* in the individual parts of the film are likewise shifted. The most astonishing thing about *Potemkin* is that the golden-section principle is observed not only with regard to the ' *zero* ' point but with regard to the culmination point as well. The latter point is the raising of the red flag on the battleship. This occurs also at a point of the golden section but in *reverse proportion* (3:2), that is, at the point dividing the first three parts from the last two — *at the end of part III.* And the flag still figures at the beginning of part IV.

Thus, we see that each individual part of the film, as well as the film on the whole, its culmination and ' zero ' points are built strictly in conformity with the principle of golden section, that is, proportionally.

Now let us consider the second distinctive characteristic of *Potemkin* — its pathos and the compositional means by which it is achieved.

We do not intend to define pathos as such. We shall confine ourselves to studying the effect a work marked with pathos produces on the spectator.

Pathos arouses deep emotions and enthusiasm.

To achieve this, such a work must be built throughout on strong explosive action and constant qualitative changes.

One and the same event may be incorporated in a work of art in different guises : in the form of a dispassionate statement or in that of a pathetic hymn. Here we are interested in the means of lifting an event to the heights of pathos.

There is no doubt that the treatment of an event is primarily determined by the author's attitude to the content. But composition, as we understand it, is the means of expressing the author's attitude and influencing the spectators.

That is why in this article we are less concerned with the nature of pathos of one or another event, for this depends on one's social viewpoint. Nor shall we touch upon the nature of *the author's attitude* to this event, for this, too, is determined by his social outlook. What we are interested in is the particular problem of what compositional means are employed to express this attitude within a work of pathos.

If we wish the spectator to experience a maximum emotional upsurge, to send him into ecstasy, we must offer him a suitable ' formula ' which will eventually excite the desirable emotions in him.

The simplest method is to present on the screen a human being in a state of ecstasy, that is, a character who is gripped by some emotion, who is ' beside himself '.

A more complicated and more effective method is the realization of the main condition of a work of pathos — constant qualitative changes in the action — not through the medium of one character, but through the entire environment. In other words, when everything around him is also ' beside itself '. A classical example of this method is the storm raging in the breast of King Lear and everywhere around him in nature.

To return to our example — the Odessa steps.

How are the events arranged and presented in this scene?

13

Leaving aside the frenzied state of the characters and masses in the scene, let us see how one of the structural and compositional means — *movement* — is used to express mounting emotional intensity.

First, there are *close-ups* of human figures rushing chaotically. Then, *long-shots* of the same scene. The *chaotic movement* is next superseded by shots showing the feet of soldiers as they march *rhythmically* down the steps.

Tempo increases. Rhythm accelerates.

And then, as the *downward* movement reaches its culmination, the movement is suddenly reversed : instead of the headlong rush of the *crowd* down the steps we see the *solitary* figure of a mother carrying her dead son, *slowly* and *solemnly going up* the steps.

Mass. Headlong rush. *Downward*. And all of a sudden —

A *solitary* figure. Slow and solemn. *Going up*. But only for a moment. Then again a *leap in the reverse direction. Downward* movement.

Rhythm accelerates. Tempo increases.

The shot of *the rushing crowd* is suddenly followed by one showing a perambulator hurtling down the steps. This is more than just different tempos. This is a *leap in the method of representation* — from the abstract to the physical. This gives one more aspect of downward movement.

Close-ups, accordingly, give place to *long shots.* The *chaotic rush* (of a mass) is succeeded by the *rhythmic* march of the soldiers. One aspect of movement (people running, falling, tumbling down the steps) gives way to another (rolling perambulator). *Descent* gives place to *ascent. Many* volleys of *many* rifles give place to *one* shot from *one* of the battleship's guns.

At each step there is a leap from one dimension to another, from one quality to another, until, finally, the change affects not one individual episode (the perambulator) but the whole of the method : the risen lions mark the point where the *narrative* turns into a *presentation through images*.

14

The visible steps of the stairs marking the downward progress of action correspond to steps marking qualitative leaps but proceeding in the opposite direction of mounting intensity.

Thus, the dramatic theme, unfolding impetuously in the scene of shooting on the steps, is at the same time the structural leit-motif, determining the plastic and rhythmical arrangement of the events.

Does the episode on the steps fit in into the organic whole? Does it disrupt the structural conception? No, it does not. The traits characteristic of a work of pathos are given here great prominence, and the episode is the tragic culmination of the entire film.

It would not be out of place to recall what I have said above about the two parts into which each of the five acts is divided in accordance with the golden-section principle. I have stressed repeatedly that action invariably leaps into a new quality at each *caesura*; now I should emphasize that the range of the new quality into which the leap is made is always the *greatest possible* : each time *the leap is into the opposite*.

We see, accordingly, that all the decisive elements of composition conform to the formula of the ecstatic : the action always makes a leap into a new quality, and this new leap is usually a leap into the opposite direction.

In this, as in the case discussed above regarding the principle of golden section and its role of determining proportions, lies the secret of organic unity as manifested in the *development* of the plot. Transition from one quality to another by means of leaps is not merely a formula of *growth* but one of *development*. We are drawn into this development not only as 'vegetative' individuals subordinated to the *evolutionary laws of nature,* but as part of collective and social units consciously participating in its development, for we know that such leaps are characteristic of social life. They

15

are the *revolutions* which stimulate social development and social movement.

We can safely say that there is a third aspect of the organic unity of *Potemkin*. The leap which characterizes the structure of each compositional element and the composition of the entire film is the compositional expression of the most important element of the theme — of the revolutionary outburst. And that is one in a series of leaps by means of which social development proceeds uninterruptedly.

The structure of a many-sided work, like that of a work of pathos, can be defined in the following words: a pathetic structure makes us *relive acutely the moments of culmination and substantiation* that are in the canon of all dialectical processes.*

Of all the living beings on earth we are alone privileged to experience and relive, one after another, the moments of the substantiation of the most important achievements in social development. More. We have the privilege of participating collectively in making a new human history.

Living through an historical moment is the culminating point of the pathos of feeling oneself part of the process, of feeling oneself part of the collective waging a fight for a bright future.

Such is pathos in life. And such is its reflection in pathetic works of art. Born of the pathos of the theme, the compositional structure echoes that basic and single law which governs the organic process — social and otherwise — involved in the making of the universe. Participation in this canon (the reflection of which is our consciousness, and its area of application — all our existence) cannot but fill us to the highest point with emotional sensation — pathos.

---

* The present article treats of one particular part of these canons. A thorough study of the problem will be dealt with in my forthcoming book for directors. — *Author's Note.*

16

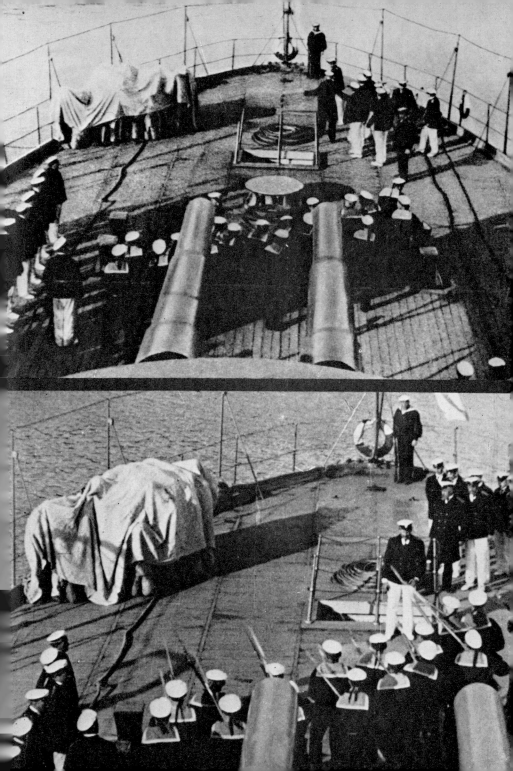

A question remains : How is the artist to achieve practically these formulas of composition? These compositional formulas are to be found in any fully pathetic work. But they are not achieved by any single compositional scheme determined *a priori*. Skill alone, craftsmanship alone, mastery alone, is not enough.

The work becomes organic and reaches the heights of genuine pathos only when the theme and content and idea of the work become an organic and continuous whole with the ideas, the feelings, with the very breath of the author.

must be organic w/ author

Then and then only will occur a genuine organic-ness of a work, which enters the circle of natural and social phenomena as a fellow-member with equal rights, as an independent phenomenon.

1939

CREDITS:

Original Russian title	Bronenosets Potemkin
Produced by	First Goskino Production, Moscow
Original story by	Nina Agadjhanova in collaboration with Sergei Eisenstein
Scenario and script	Sergei Eisenstein
Directed by	Sergei Eisenstein
Photography	Eduard Tisse
Assistant Director	Grigory Alexandrov
Assistants to Eisenstein	A. Antonov, A. Levshin, M. Gomorov, M. Shtrauk, L. Kryukov
Producer	Jacob Bliokh
Editor	Sergei Eisenstein
Art Director	Vasili Rakhals
Camera Assistant	V. Popov
Sub titles	Nikolai Asseyev (poet born in 1889)
Sound	Silent film, background music by Nikolai Kryukov
Original musical score	Edmund Meisel
Length	1,640 metres
Shot during	July-November 1925
Locations	Leningrad, at Odessa and aboard the *Twelve Apostles* (the sister-ship of the *Prince Potemkin of Taurida*) which was put aground in the Bay of Sevastopol
Edited	November-December 1925 in Moscow

CAST:

Vakulinchuk	A. Antonov
Commander Golikov	Vladimir Barsky
Senior Officer Gilyarovsky	Grigory Alexandrov
Sailor Matyushenko	M. Gomorov
Ship's Surgeon Smirnov	An anonymous workman
Priest	An anonymous old gardener from the orchards on the outskirts of Sevastopol
Boatswain	Levchenko
Woman on the steps	Repnikova
Officer	Marusov
Recruits	I. Bobrov and A. Fait
Others	Sailors of the Red Navy
	Citizens of Odessa
	Members of the Proletcult Theatre

First showing	21st December 1925 at the Bolshoi Theatre in Moscow
General release in Russia	16th January 1926

23

POTEMKIN

PART ONE: MEN AND MAGGOTS

A huge wave breaks violently over the jetty, raising a sparkling fountain of spray, and

. . . flows turbulently over the stones on the shore.

Wave after wave breaks over the jetty, ever more violently, and

. . . flows over the stones on the shore, ever more turbulently. The raging sea boils.

REVOLUTION MEANS WAR. THIS — THIS IS THE ONE LAWFUL, REASONABLE AND JUST, TRULY GREAT WAR OF ALL THE WARS THAT HISTORY HAS KNOWN. IN RUSSIA THIS WAR HAS BEEN DECLARED AND BEGUN . . .*

Its stark, geometrical beauty distinguishing it, a powerful battleship lies in the anchorage.

On the battleship, a sailor ascends a ladder. He is quickly approached by another.

THE SAILORS MATYUSHENKO AND VAKULIN-CHUK . . .

Matyushenko speaks urgently to Vakulinchuk:

'*We, the sailors of the Potemkin, must support the workers, our brothers, and must stand in the front ranks of the revolution.*'

Vakulinchuk answers him in agitation and quickly descends the ladder.

By night, the silhouette of the battleship stands out starkly and majestically in the anchorage.

---

* *Lenin: Collected Works, Vol. 9, p. 212.*

THE OFF-DUTY WATCH IN DEEP SLEEP . . .

The lower deck: packed like sardines in a tin, the sleeping sailors lie in canvas hammocks.
They sleep in uncomfortable positions and breathe noisily.
One sleeping sailor,
. . . another,
. . . a third,
. . . a fourth,
. . . a fifth.
A fat boatswain with a brutal face descends the ladder into the lower deck and looks with malice at
. . . the sleeping sailors.
He threads his way through the canvas hammocks and
. . . mistrustfully surveys
. . . the sleeping sailors.
He allows his gaze to rest
. . . on one of the sleeping men.
Continuing to thread his way through the canvas hammocks,
. . . he shifts his gaze quickly from one sleeping sailor to another.

VIGILANT, BUT CLUMSY . . .

Unexpectedly, he slips and almost falls.

HE VENTS HIS ANGER ON A YOUNG MAN . . .

Furiously, the boatswain raises his arm and
. . . lashes the naked back of a young sailor with his pipe-chain.
The young sailor awakens, looks uncomprehendingly at the boatswain
. . . and speaks out in surprise.
The boatswain looks impudently at the young sailor and plays with the chain.
The young sailor, stiff with rage and resentment, stares hotly

. . . at the departing boatswain,
. . . turns over with hatred,
. . . and throws his face violently against his pillow.
The muscles of his naked back twitch.

INDIGNANTLY . . .

His neighbour lays a sympathetic hand on his shoulder and points out to him the figure of Vakulinchuk on one side.

VAKULINCHUK . . .

Amidst the canvas hammocks, naked to the waist, Vakulinchuk, holding a leaflet in his hand, speaks with passion and resolution to the sailors :
' *Comrades, the time has come when we must speak out.*'
Vakulinchuk's whole body breathes hatred.
The sailors awaken
. . . one by one.
Vakulinchuk turns to the sailors with the appeal :
' *What are we waiting for? All Russia has risen. Are we to be the last?* '
He continues his speech passionately.
A sailor with a sickly face assents to everything he says,
. . . and a sailor with a big moustache impatiently interrupts him and demands the beginning of action.
Again, the sailor with the sickly face utters a few fighting words.
Firmly and manfully, Vakulinchuk calls for battle.
Again, the sailor with the big moustache demands the beginning of action.
All the sailors listen with attention and fellow-feeling to the words of Vakulinchuk.

MORNING . . .

A gloomy-looking officer, his hands in his pockets, walks along the deck. Suddenly he notices that

. . . a crowd of sailors have gathered around a carcass of meat.
The crowd of sailors grows larger
. . . and larger.
A senior officer with a proud, weakly aristocratic face steps
out of a cabin, and,
. . . pompously, his hands clasped behind his back, begins to
walk along the deck,
. . . but he soon stops and
. . . looks contemptuously
. . . at the sailors surging around the carcass of meat.
The eyes of the senior officer fill with malice when he notices
the figure of Vakulinchuk walking past the carcass of meat.
The crowd of sailors excitedly inspect the carcass of meat.
The senior officer moves away and
. . . soon reappears on the upper deck, above the heads of the
sailors.
The legs of the approaching senior officer draw near to the
handrail.
The senior officer looks at the sailors with such menace that
. . . they timidly press closer to one another. The legs of the
officer turn away.
The senior officer goes off, and the crowd of sailors surges
with ever-increasing movement.
' *We've had enough of eating rotten meat!* '
Again, the faces of the sailors turn with indignation to inspect
the carcass of rotten meat. (*Still on page 17*)
The indignation of the sailors grows.
' *A dog wouldn't eat it!* '
Again and again, the faces of the sailors turn to inspect the
carcass of rotten meat.
The crowd of sailors around the carcass bubbles like a whirl-
pool.
The senior officer returns — with the ship's surgeon, a small
short-sighted man, his courage comically mustered.
With an authoritative expression, the surgeon examines and

sniffs at the carcass of rotten meat,
. . . turning it over squeamishly.
Vakulinchuk, standing in front of the sailors, indignantly points out the rotten meat to the surgeon.

SHIP'S SURGEON SMIRNOV . . .

The surgeon heatedly rebuts Vakulinchuk,
. . . but Vakulinchuk says bitterly :
' It's so high it could walk overboard! '
Vakulinchuk looks angrily at the surgeon.
The surgeon slowly and importantly removes his pince-nez,
. . . folds its two eye-pieces together,
. . . raises them to his eye,
. . . and examines the meat through the folded eye-pieces of his pince-nez.
The meat is visibly infested with maggots.
However, the surgeon does not agree with Vakulinchuk that the meat is rotten,
. . . and agitatedly waves his pince-nez about.
' These are not maggots.'
Through the folded eye-pieces of the surgeon's pince-nez, it is evident that the meat is swarming with large maggots.
Vakulinchuk and the sailors look with fury at the heartless, typically Tsarist official, as loathsome himself as a maggot.
The surgeon, having assumed an air of indifference, replaces his pince-nez and, rolling his eyes, says sharply and dryly to the sailors :
' They are the dead larvae of flies. They can be washed off with vinegar.'
He speaks peremptorily, cutting the air with his forefinger.
Then, carefully and fastidiously, he raises the end of the carcass and turns to the senior officer for support.
He swings the end of the carcass.
The senior officer, interesting himself in the meat, also raises the end of the carcass — carefully and fastidiously.

31

Vakulinchuk knocks the end of the carcass out of the surgeon's hand and says angrily to him :
' *Russian prisoners-of-war in Japan eat better than us!* '
. . . and, pointing at the rotten, maggoty meat, he shouts :
' *We've had enough of eating rotten meat!* '
The surgeon walks away hurriedly,
. . . trying to pacify the sailors.
The senior officer also tries to soothe the sailors, but he quickly
. . . joins the enraged surgeon.
The surgeon, breaking into a violent frenzy, shouts :
' *The meat is good. There's nothing more to be said.*'
Continuing to shout angrily, he stands very erect,
. . . his hands by the side of his uniform, but,
. . . suddenly, from fear, his head sinks deeply into his shoulders when he sees
. . . the sailors, Vakulinchuk at their head, moving quickly and boldly forwards.
Helplessly, the surgeon jerks up his shoulders, and looks for assistance to the senior officer,
. . . who maintains a proud and majestic pose.
Frightened, the surgeon
. . . scurries round the back of the senior officer.
The senior officer, frozen in his proud and majestic pose, watches contemptuously
. . . as the sailors approach.
The senior officer calmly and slowly turns his back on them,
. . . and moves further away with the surgeon.
Confidently, the sailors follow them.
The senior officer and the surgeon depart quickly,
. . . and the sailors drop back.
The sailors continue to crowd around the carcass of meat. A malicious, fierce-faced officer appears and
. . . begins to shout at the sailors.

SENIOR OFFICER GILYAROVSKY . . .

32

Officer Gilyarovsky roughly disperses the crowd of sailors. Furiously, he swears at them and
. . . shouts.

Then he goes up to the boatswain, who proceeds himself to drive the sailors away from the carcass of meat.

A fat cook sniffs squeamishly at the carcass of rotten, maggoty meat and bears it off.

In the ship's galley, he begins
. . . to hack at the carcass with an axe.

Sailors indignantly approach and tell him that the meat is rotten, but he does not stop hacking at the carcass.

More sailors approach and try to prevent him from hacking at the rotten meat.

The axe hacks the carcass into pieces.

The sailors try to tear the rotten meat from him, but he swears at them and
. . . continues his work.

The axe hacks the carcass into pieces.

On deck, the muzzle of a cannon is being cleaned.

Seated on the muzzle, a sailor cleans it.

A cleaning-rod is pushed down the muzzle of the cannon.

Two sailors polish a copper capstan.

Again, a cleaning-rod is pushed down the muzzle of the cannon.

The sailor on the muzzle withdraws the cleaning-rod.

Two sailors polish a copper capstan.

Two sailors polish some copper engine-parts.

A third pair of sailors clean a chain.

Two sailors polish a copper capstan.

One of the two sailors cleaning the chain stops work and begins to converse with his comrade.

Borshch from the rotten meat bubbles in a cauldron.

In the ship's mess a detachment of sailors begin

. . . to let down the tables which hang by ropes from the ceiling.

One file of sailors leaves the ship's mess,

. . . and, then, another.

Borshch from the rotten meat bubbles in a cauldron.

The fat boatswain with the brutal face enters, playing with his pipe-chain,

. . . and walks between the empty tables which swing rhythmically on ropes from the ceiling, and,

. . . with an important air, he stops and gives his orders.

Some sailors begin to arrange tureens on the tables.

The tables with the tureens upon them swing rhythmically on ropes from the ceiling.

Borshch from the rotten meat bubbles in a cauldron.

Some sailors can be seen through a grating.

A group of sailors sit by the edge of one side of the battleship. One of them, holding a dried fish in his hand, talks indignantly.

Another cuts off a piece of black bread.

The sailor with the fish is full of anger and hatred.

IMPOTENT FURY SWEEPS OVER THE GROUP OF SAILORS . . .

The sailor with the fish fits the head of it beneath a ring on the deck and

. . . forcefully

. . tears it off.

Some sailors can be seen through a grating.

A pile of salt on a rag and a hunk of black bread.

One young sailor snaps off a piece of black bread and chews it for his dinner.

Mugs are filled with fresh water from taps.

Near the pile of salt on the rag and the hunk of black bread — a mug of water.

One young sailor chews, and drinks water from the mug.

34

As soon as the young sailor finishes drinking, he sprinkles salt on the bread, and his neighbour takes the mug and drinks.
Senior officer Gilyarovsky descends the ladder into the ship's mess.
Several sailors stand to attention, but do not salute him.
A young sailor salutes, and
. . . Gilyarovsky carelessly waves his hand.
Frowning at Gilyarovsky, the young sailor lowers his hand.
A wicked expression on his face, Gilyarovsky appears to consider something.
The sailors do not meet his eyes and
. . . quickly go out, one
. . . after another.
A smile of malicious triumph appears on Gilyarovsky's face.
He turns sharply and
. . . moves rapidly between the tables.
The tables with the tureens upon them swing rhythmically on ropes from the ceiling.
Gilyarovsky stops by a cupboard, opens the door of it, and inclines his head.
The tables with the tureens upon them swing rhythmically on ropes from the ceiling.
Gilyarovsky shakes his head significantly.
A table laid with empty tureens and with black bread upon it swings rhythmically on ropes from the ceiling.
Indignant, Gilyarovsky
. . . quickly walks out of the ship's mess.

THE SHIP'S STORE . . .

Some sailors stand by the little window of the ship's store, buying food.
In the window
. . . tins of food
. . . appear fleetingly
. . . in the hands of the sailors.

35

One of the sailors sees Gilyarovsky approaching.
Gilyarovsky looks wickedly
. . . at the sailors.
His gaze fixes tensely upon them, but he turns quickly and departs.
The sailors follow Gilyarovsky with their eyes. When he is no longer in sight, they continue
. . . to buy food.
On the captain's bridge, the senior officer with the weakly aristocratic face looks through his binoculars. Gilyarovsky goes up to him and reports on the behaviour of the sailors. Together, they descend the ladder,
. . . enter the ship's mess.
. . . and walk between the suspended tables,
. . . considering the situation which has developed.
A table laid with empty tureens and with black bread upon it swings rhythmically on ropes from the ceiling.
The two senior officers, conversing all the while,
. . . begin
. . . to ascend
. . . the ladder.
The sailors talk uneasily among themselves.
The senior officer enters the room next to the ship's galley and
. . . gives orders to the cook.
The cook opens the door to the galley, and the cooking range in the galley becomes visible,
. . . and the saucepans,
. . . and the other cook at work.
The senior officer completes his orders to the first cook.
The second cook walks out of the galley, salutes and
. . . reports to the senior officer.
The senior officer angrily upbraids the first cook.
When the second cook has reported,
. . . the senior officer departs.
A young sailor is washing some plates,

36

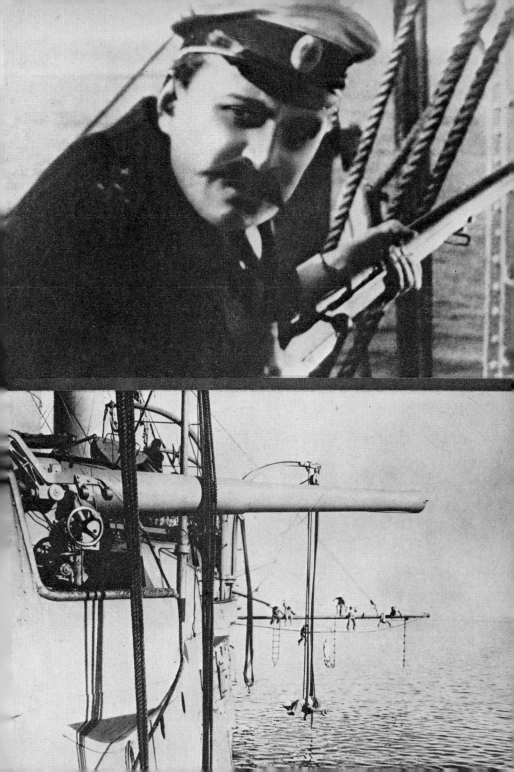

. . . and another, painstakingly, dries them.

Dinner for the 'gentlemen officers' is being prepared.

The washing and the drying of plates goes on.

With a characteristic movement, the young sailor washing the plates wipes his nose with his hand.

He continues to wash the plates,

. . . a second sailor — to lay the table for dinner,

. . . the third — painstakingly to dry the plates.

The young sailor washing the plates continues to hand them to

. . . the other young sailor who, painstakingly, dries them.

The young sailor washes an earthenware plate, on the rim of which is a circular inscription.

He is whistling,

. . . but the inscription on the plate attracts his attention.

He leans his head towards the plate and

. . . begins slowly to turn it in his hands.

Moving his head from one side to the other,

. . . he reads the circular inscription: ' *Give us this day* . . .'

. . . and he repeats these words aloud.

Continuing to revolve the plate in his hands, he reads further from the inscription on its rim: '. . . *our daily bread.*'

His face breaks into a scowl.

He begins carefully to examine

. . . the inscription on the plate.

Involuntarily repeating the words aloud, he looks with loathing at

. . . the inscription on the plate,

. . . and becomes thoughtful.

Revolving the plate rapidly in his hands,

. . . he looks intently at it and

. . . bitterly pronounces the words of the inscription.

He raises the plate high and,

. . . having swept his hands down

. . . and up,

. . . he hurls it
. . . violently
. . . down
. . . and smashes it to pieces against the table.
The young sailor straightens up and sees that
. . . the covers on the table for the dinner of the ' gentlemen
officers ' have been upset.

PART TWO: DRAMA ON THE QUARTER-DECK

The bugle sounds
... shrilly and uneasily.
Seen from above — past the muzzles of the cannons menacingly overhanging — the sailors quickly fill the quarter-deck, forming themselves in double file along either side of the deck. At the prow of the battleship the flag of St. Andrew flutters in the wind.
The bugler sounds his call.
The petty officers arrange themselves in single file in front of the sailors.
A group of officers fall in behind the hatch in the middle of the deck.

COMMANDER GOLIKOV ...

From the hatch appears the figure of Commander Golikov, resolutely ascending the ladder.
The officers salute him.
Commander Golikov steps onto the deck and
... salutes.
He walks up to a capstan and
... stands upon it.
The sailors in their ranks stand stiffly to attention,
... and so do the petty officers. (*Still on page 18*)
Nobody stirs. The muzzles of the cannons hang menacingly over the ranks.
Commander Golikov, one hand by the side of his frock-coat, the other behind his back, looks threateningly round the motionless rows of sailors.
The officers are at the salute.
Restraining his fury, Commander Golikov orders:
'*Those satisfied with the borshch* ——'

43

A pause.

'—— *two paces forward!*'

He raises an admonishing hand.

A number of petty officers step hesitantly forward.

THE PETTY OFFICERS . . .

The petty officers who have kept rank falter. After a while, one of them takes two steps forward.

The officers stand motionless, at the salute.

Only two of the petty officers have kept rank. . . . Whereupon, two of the sailors break rank and step forward.

Commander Golikov, one hand by the side of his frock-coat, the other behind his back, looks threateningly about him.

A young petty officer, not knowing what to do, mechanically fingers the strap running over his shoulder.

The muzzles of the cannons hang menacingly over a motionless rank of sailors.

The senior petty officer looks apprehensively at the men who have not moved.

'*Come on!*'

The young petty officer, not knowing what to do, mechanically fingers the strap running over his shoulder.

Enraged, Commander Golikov shouts:

'*Hang the rest on the yard-arm!*'

. . . and he points

. . . at the mast.

A young officer with a small moustache, turning his eyes in the direction of the mast, can hardly repress a smile.

The words of the Commander strike terror in the hearts of the sailors.

They turn their heads in the direction of the mast.

Before the eyes of one old sailor, there begins to swim

. . . the vision of the sailors hanging on the yard-arm.

The old sailor looks fearfully in the direction of the mast.

The two petty officers turn their eyes towards

44

. . . the mast.
One of the petty officers turns towards the other with a nervous smile.
Commander Golikov shakes his hand threateningly.
The tensely smiling face of the petty officer immediately becomes serious.
Commander Golikov fixes his eyes ominously on the sailors.
The petty officer is stiff with fright.
Commander Golikov shouts :
' *Call out the guard!* '
. . . and does not remove his gaze from the sailors.
Seen from above — past the muzzles of the cannons menacingly overhanging — a sailor breaks rank and quickly runs past the gun-turret.

MATYUSHENKO BREAKS RANK AND EDGES TOWARDS THE GUN-TURRET . . .

Matyushenko exhorts the sailors.
The sailor returns and runs quickly up to the Commander.
Matyushenko says to the sailors :
' *To the turret* ',
. . . and he points at the gun-turret.
The sailors convey the message one to another :
' *To the turret.* '
Matyushenko directs the sailors :
' *To the turret.* '
The sailors quickly convey Matyushenko's direction one to another.
The sailors in rank, their faces gloomy, stand motionless.
Seen from above — past the muzzles of the cannons menacingly overhanging — the armed guard, dressed in black uniforms, move past the gun-turret.
Two evil-faced officers converse agitatedly.
Beneath the muzzles of the cannons menacingly overhanging, past the ranks of sailors, the guard move, rifles in hand.

The officers exchange glances with one another significantly.
The guard pass by the ranks of sailors
. . . and fall into line in front of the Commander.
Matyushenko turns to the sailors :
' Lads . . .'
He shouts :
' It is time! '
The sailors break rank and,
. . . quickly,
. . . according to Matyushenko's direction,
. . . race towards
. . . the gun-turret.

MOST OF THE SAILORS ARE GATHERED BY THE GUN-TURRET . . .

Seen from above — past the muzzles of the cannons menacingly overhanging — most of the sailors have gathered by the gun-turret,
. . . and only a small knot of sailors remain on the prow of the battleship.
From this knot of sailors, a number detach themselves and run towards the gun-turret.
Senior officer Gilyarovsky frowns viciously.
The crowd of sailors is agitated.
Gilyarovsky, raising his hand, shouts at the sailors remaining on the prow of the battleship :
' Stop! Into rank! '
The sailors remaining on the prow of the battleship look in terror (*Still on page 18*)
. . . at the infuriated Gilyarovsky, and
. . . try to run towards the gun-turret, but they are driven back by the officers.
The captain of the guard awaits the orders of the Commander.

THEY TRY TO MAKE THEIR WAY THROUGH THE ADMIRAL'S HATCH . . .

Some of the sailors remaining on the prow of the battleship advance towards the admiral's hatch.

Commander Golikov shouts at them in fury:

' Back, you villains! This is no way for you! '

. . . and he springs at the sailors with his fists,

. . . catches one of them, and

. . . hurls him at the feet of the other sailors, and then

. . . catches another.

The sailors raise their fallen comrade.

Commander Golikov shouts at the sailors in fury:

' I'll shoot you like dogs! '

. . . and he shakes his fist threateningly.

The sailor looks bitterly at him and

. . . rejoins his comrades.

Senior officer Gilyarovsky

. . . commands the guard to turn about towards the sailors remaining on the prow of the battleship,

. . . climbs up onto the capstan,

. . . and, with a triumphant smirk, orders:

' Cover them with a tarpaulin! '

Three petty officers break rank.

' Aye, aye, sir.'

They come to a halt,

. . . salute,

. . . then turn and

. . . go back, one

. . . after another. Two more petty officers follow them.

A triumphant smirk on his lips, Gilyarovsky twirls his moustache.

The petty officers take hold of a tarpaulin.

Gilyarovsky continues to twirl his moustache.

The petty officers

. . . carry the tarpaulin

. . . past the guard. One of the sailors in the guard turns his head and looks dejectedly at the tarpaulin.

The petty officers continue to carry the tarpaulin past the guard.

The sailor in the guard who had looked at the tarpaulin turns his head back and stands upright.

The petty officers carry the tarpaulin past the guard.

The sailor in the guard dejectedly lowers his head.

The petty officers with the tarpaulin draw close to the sailors remaining on the prow of the battleship, throw the tarpaulin down on to the deck and begin to unroll it.

The sailors gathered by the gun-turret follow tensely the actions of the petty officers and the guard.

'Cover them!'

The petty officers unroll

. . . the tarpaulin.

The knot of sailors remaining on the prow of the battleship press themselves in terror against the handrail of the deck, covering their faces with their hands.

The petty officers raise

. . . the tarpaulin

. . . and cover the sailors with it.

The tarpaulin

. . . covers the sailors.

The guard stand motionless, rifles at ease.

An officer approaches.

' Attention!'

The file of petty officers

. . . and the officers

. . . brace themselves.

The sailors in the guard stiffen.

The guard stand in front of the knot of sailors covered with the tarpaulin. Gilyarovsky runs up to the guard.

The muzzles of the cannons look menacingly down.

The reflection of the battleship dances on the waves.

The ship's priest appears on the deck and raises his hands to the sky.

'*Lord, let these sinners understand.*'
Some of the sailors covered with the tarpaulin fall to their knees. (*Still on page 19*)
The priest raises his cross and speaks.
Senior officer Gilyarovsky orders :
'*At the tarpaulin — aim!*'
The sailors in the guard load, and
. . . raise their rifles (*Still on page 19*)
. . . to the shoulder.
The sailors in the guard consider with horror the imminent shooting of the knot of sailors covered with the tarpaulin and
. . . lower their heads.
Several of the sailors covered with the tarpaulin are on their knees.
The heads of the sailors in the guard are dejectedly lowered, but,
. . . on the command,
. . . the sailors raise their rifles to the shoulder.
Three officers look on tensely.
The priest, counting off the seconds, mechanically slaps his cross against his palm
. . . several times. (*Still on page 20*)
The face of a young petty officer twitches with fear. Tormentedly counting off the tense seconds, he strokes the knife in his belt.
Gilyarovsky shouts furiously.
Almost all the sailors covered with the tarpaulin have fallen to their knees.
Standing in a row, the officers are motionless.
The sailors in the guard level the muzzles of their rifles
. . . and aim at the knot of sailors covered with the tarpaulin.
The sailors standing near the gun-turret look on with terror
. . . as the guard aim their rifles at the knot of sailors covered with the tarpaulin.
The priest slaps his cross several times more against his palm.

49

It is as if time had stopped . . . the deathly hush before the storm.

On a life-belt, the clear inscription: *'Prince Potemkin Tavrichesky.'*

The prow of the battleship — with a Tsarist eagle.

The bugler holds his bugle in readiness.

The tension is at its peak. Vakulinchuk makes a decisive movement.

VAKULINCHUK DECIDES . . .

Gilyarovsky orders the guard:
'Fire!'
Vakulinchuk shouts to the guard:
'Brothers!'
With horror on his face, he again shouts to the guard:
'Who are you shooting at?'
A sailor in the guard continues to take aim.

THE RIFLES WAVER . . .

Several sailors in the guard lower their rifles. The incident has reached crisis point.

Gilyarovsky, raising his fists, shouts at the guard in fury:
'Shoot!'
One after another, the sailors in the guard lower their rifles.
One of the sailors in the guard does not know what to do.
'Shoot!'
His fists flying, Gilyarovsky throws himself
. . . at the guard who have refused to shoot at the sailors on the prow of the battleship,
. . . and he shouts:
'Shoot, you villains!'
The priest, his cross raised, stiffens with terror.
Gilyarovsky's face is distorted with rage. *(Still on page 38)*
The sailors in the guard,
. . . one after another,

. . . return their rifles to the position at ease,
. . . or lower the muzzles. (*Still on page 37*)
Again Gilyarovsky shouts,
. . . and hurls himself at the guard with his fists,
. . . and tries to snatch one of the sailor's rifles.
Matyushenko shouts to the sailors : (*Still on page 37*)
' *Seize the rifles, comrades!* '
He races to get a rifle.
Gilyarovsky snatches the sailor's rifle.
Vakulinchuk gives orders to the sailors.
The storm has burst. Sailors race for the rifles.
Sailors encircle Gilyarovsky.
Vakulinchuk shouts to the sailors :
' *Smash the dragons! Smash them!* '
He shouts again :
' *Smash every one of them!* '
He continues to shout.
The sailors remaining on the prow of the battleship fling off
the tarpaulin and
. . . run towards
. . . the group of officers.
The sailors encircle the officers.
One sailor tries to snatch Gilyarovsky's rifle.
The sailors on the prow of the battleship, having flung off
the tarpaulin, run quickly.
Sailors in the guard raise their rifles.
The tarpaulin, picked up by the wind, descends slowly to the
deck.
The sailors knock the officers down
. . . and attack them.
Sailors with rifles run rapidly around the upper deck.
The flag of St Andrew flutters
. . . above the fighting on the battleship.
The sailors attack the officers
. . . and the Commander.

51

Sailors with rifles run rapidly around the decks.
Sailors rush to the armoury,
... and one of them
... quickly dispenses rifles
... to the sailors who come running up,
... one
... after another
... without interruption.
Gilyarovsky and Commander Golikov start to descend the admiral's hatch, but Golikov is seized by sailors.
Elsewhere, sailors attack an officer.
Golikov throws off the sailors.
The sailors knock the officer down onto the tarpaulin.
Elsewhere, Matyushenko, with other sailors, attacks a group of petty officers.
The flag of St Andrew flutters.
Near the admiral's hatch, the young officer with the small moustache repels the sailors' attacks.
Sailors with rifles run rapidly around the decks.
The sailors roll the officer up in the tarpaulin.
Rifles,
... one
... after another,
... are passed through
... a grille
... to the sailors who come running up.
The sailors roll the officer up in the tarpaulin.
Gilyarovsky, armed with a rifle, chases after Vakulinchuk.
Vakulinchuk climbs across a circular bastion and lets himself drop,
... trying to hide from him.
From a hatch protrudes a hand with a crucifix,
... standing out clearly against the background of the grating.
Vakulinchuk, raising himself slightly, grasps the handrail near the hatch.

From the hatch appears the figure of the priest, cross in hand, ascending the ladder.

Vakulinchuk looks at him uncomprehendingly.

The priest speaks to him :

' *Fear God,* '

. . . and stretches out the cross to him.

The crucifix stands out against the background of the grating.

Matyushenko and his comrades attack the officers.

Vakulinchuk shouts at the priest :

' *Get out of the way, you sorcerer!* '

. . . and he pushes him

. . . down.

Running up, Gilyarovsky raises the butt of his rifle against Vakulinchuk,

. . . but Vakulinchuk seizes the rifle and tries to tear it from him.

The sailors roll the officer up in the tarpaulin. He resists, clutching at a ring on the deck.

Vakulinchuk and Gilyarovsky fight for possession of the rifle. The officer lets go of the ring. The sailors drag him away from it.

For a moment appear the legs of Vakulinchuk and Gilyarovsky, fighting for possession of the rifle.

Vakulinchuk runs down the ladder, but, again,

. . . for a moment appear the legs

. . . of Vakulinchuk and Gilyarovsky, fighting for possession of the rifle.

On the deck, the crowd of sailors continues to attack the officers.

The priest, stepping out of the hatch, extends his cross to Vakulinchuk. At that moment, Gilyarovsky seizes the rifle from Vakulinchuk.

The crucifix falls

. . . and sticks upright into the floor of the deck.

The priest falls

... into the hatch
... and, hitting his head against a pipe, loses consciousness. Vakulinchuk
... quickly runs down
... the ladder into the hatch,
... chased by Gilyarovsky.
Vakulinchuk turns, sees
... the crucifix stuck into the floor of the deck, and
... runs on.
Through the ship's galley an officer runs,
... seeking safety from the sailors.
Up onto the wardroom piano
... an officer clambers, struggling with the sailors pursuing him.
He treads on the keys
... and on the candelabra,
... and, having got on top of the piano, he fires his revolver at the sailors,
... but the sailors pursuing him drag him down from the piano,
... upturning him.
An officer hangs by his hands from the muzzle of a cannon.
In the wardroom, the sailors beat the officer against the floor. On one side of the battleship, an officer notices a sailor swarming along a ladder in pursuit of him.
The officer, seeking safety from the sailor, clambers up the side of the battleship, clutching at the holdfasts, but the sailor's leg kicks him over the head. The officer clambers back, and the sailor descends after him.
In the wardroom, the sailors continue
... to attack the officer.
Two sailors run up the ladder to a hatch.
On the side of the battleship, the sailor, descending by the holdfasts, again kicks the officer over the head.

In the wardroom, a sailor attacks the officer with a music-stool.

Hanging over the arm of a chair, only the hand of the dead officer can be seen.

On the side of the battleship, the sailor propels

. . . the officer into the sea. (*Still on page 40*)

The water receives the officer greedily.

On a life-belt, the clear inscription: ' *Prince Potemkin Tavrichesky.*'

Sailors with rifles run rapidly around the decks.

With the butt of his rifle,

. . . a sailor attacks

. . . an officer who has run to the end of the muzzle of a cannon.

The officer loses balance,

. . . somersaults in the air,

. . . and falls

. . . into the sea,

. . . where he struggles to get out.

Smirnov, the small, short-sighted ship's surgeon, tries to conceal himself behind a row of hose-pipes,

. . . but he is detected

. . . and encircled by sailors,

. . . who drag him away.

He clings helplessly to a rope.

The sailors try to tear him from the rope,

. . . and they carry him away,

. . . head downwards,

. . . the rope trailing after him,

. . . down a metal ladder. In his deathly fear

. . . he clutches with his hands at the steps.

The priest, fallen into the hatch, opens one eye for an instant and closes it.

Smirnov clings with his hands to the steps.

On the ladder, the legs

. . . of the sailors and of the struggling officer.
On the deck, sailors with rifles hunt down the fleeing officers.
Ship's surgeon Smirnov
. . . is snatched up by a couple of sailors.
With a swing, they hurl him
. . . overboard.
Head downwards, he flies through the air and
. . . falls into the sea,
. . . raising a fountain of spray and
. . . foam.

*GO AND FEED YOUR MAGGOTS AT THE BOTTOM
OF THE SEA . . . !*

And on a cable hang the pince-nez of ship's surgeon Smirnov
— those same pince-nez through which, with indifference, he
regarded the maggoty meat.
On the deck, the sailors continue to attack the officers.
'Comrades! The ship is in our hands!'
The sailors on the deck throw their caps high in the air with
joy.
The smashed keys of the piano: evidence of the struggle in
the wardroom.
On the decks, the sailors continue to hunt down the officers.

*FLOWING WITH BLOOD, VAKULINCHUK SEEKS
SAFETY FROM THE BESTIAL GILYAROVSKY . . .*

Gilyarovsky watches closely,
. . . as Vakulinchuk climbs onto a yard-arm.
. . . and moves along it.
Gilyarovsky, his rifle in his hand, draws closer to Vakulinchuk,
. . . not once lowering his gaze from him.
Vakulinchuk looks at Gilyarovsky.
Gilyarovsky turns,
. . . takes cover behind a buttress,
. . . aims with his rifle

56

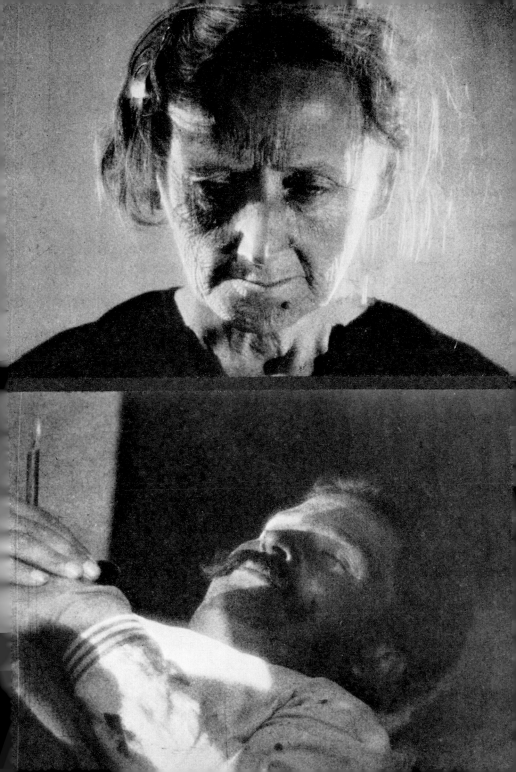

. . . at Vakulinchuk on the yard-arm,
. . . carefully screwing up one eye,
. . . and he fires.
Vakulinchuk clutches the back of his head with his hand.
Gilyarovsky looks at Vakulinchuk.
Vakulinchuk, mortally wounded, falls from the yard-arm and,
. . . catching hold of some ropes,
. . . slips down the ropes
. . . into the cradle they form above the sea.
The sailors on the deck throw their caps high in the air with
joy.
The ropes descend on a pulley, and
. . . the unconscious Vakulinchuk slips down towards the sea
in the cradle they form.
A sailor shouts:
' *Vakulinchuk's overboard!* '
. . . and runs along the yard-arm,
. . . followed by a second sailor, and a third.
Grasping the ropes,
. . . they hasten to the aid of Vakulinchuk.
Vakulinchuk lies on his back in the cradle of ropes, his head
hanging down. (*Still on page 39*)
' *Save Vakulinchuk!* '
The sailors jump into the water.
Vakulinchuk hangs over the cradle of ropes above the water,
. . . and he falls into the sea.
The sailors quickly swim
. . . towards the sinking Vakulinchuk.
The sailors slowly carry
. . . the body of the dead Vakulinchuk up the gangway.

AND HE WHO WAS THE FIRST TO TAKE UP THE
CRY OF REBELLION WAS THE FIRST TO FALL AT
THE HAND OF THE EXECUTIONER . . .

A cutter, with sailors in file on either side of the deck and

with the body of Vakulinchuk on high,
. . . moves

. . . *TOWARDS THE SHORE* . . .

The passage of the cutter, with the body of Vakulinchuk, hero
and victim of the rebellion, on high
. . . gives impetus
. . . and intensity
. . . to the noble spirit of mourning and triumph which
prevails.

ODESSA . . .

On the still quay in the moonlight : a solitary tent.

THE TENT AT THE END OF ODESSA'S NEW JETTY —VAKULINCHUK'S LAST RESTING PLACE . . .

In the tent lies the body of Vakulinchuk.
An inscription on a sheet of paper : ' *On account of a spoon-ful of borshch.* '
In his hands is a lighted candle. His body is turned towards
the town, which is visible in the distance through the opening
in the tent.
First, the cutter passes before the tent,
. . . then a large sailing-ship heading in a different direction
floats by and obscures the view of the town.

PART THREE: THE DEAD MAN CRIES FOR VENGEANCE

Moonlight plays upon the water.

MIST SWIRLS UP FROM THE NIGHT . . .

In the bay,
. . . ships
. . . wrapped in thick mist.
The turgid waves splash gently.
Seagulls on a buoy, alarmed, take wing.
The turgid waves splash gently.
The bay
. . . is full
. . . of ships.
Dawn. Beyond the corpse of Vakulinchuk, in whose hands a
lighted candle burns, can be seen the distant town.
A flag of mourning flutters on top of the tent.
Near the tent, absorbed and indifferent, a fisherman fishes
from the jetty.
A large, ocean-going vessel towers above.

*VOICES FROM THE JETTY MAKE THEMSELVES
HEARD THROUGH THE MIST . . .*

Poorly dressed men and women and children
. . . begin to move towards the tent containing the body of
Vakulinchuk.
Beyond the corpse of Vakulinchuk, the lighted candle in his
hands, the town can be seen in the distance.
An old woman enters the tent and straightens the lighted
candle in Vakulinchuk's hands. *(Still on page 57)*
All who approach, approach the tent — men and women.

63

Insensible to everything, two fishermen fish.
The lighted candle
. . . in the hands of the dead Vakulinchuk. (*Still on page 57*)
The crowd around the tent quickly grows larger. Two noble-
women, wearing expensive white dresses and carrying elegant
white umbrellas, peep curiously into the tent.
The sails of a nearby ship are put up.

*AND TOGETHER WITH THE SUN THE NEWS
BREAKS ON THE TOWN . . . !*

At first empty, the long, narrow steps leading down to the
harbour quickly fill with moving people.

THE BATTLESHIP IN THE ANCHORAGE . . .

The multitude descends
. . . the long, narrow steps.

THE REBELLION . . .

Along the bridge,
. . . quietly and purposefully,
. . . flows the stream of people. (*Still on page 59*)

THE SHORE . . .

Along the harbour
. . . flows the stream of people.

THE MURDERED SAILOR . . .

The crowd around the tent containing the body of Vakulin-
chuk quickly grows. Men and women regard the murdered
man, then pass on.
A small boy walks past the corpse of Vakulinchuk and places
a coin in the sailor's cap lying on a barrel.
In the hands of Vakulinchuk, the candle burns.
The sailor's cap on the barrel is filled with coins.
Near the tent, a student delivers a fiery speech.
Along the jetty

. . . flows the vast stream of people. (*Still on page 59*)
The multitude descends the long, narrow steps by the bridge.
The endless stream of people flows along the jetty.
Descending by both the steps which lead from the bridge to
the harbour, the stream of people
. . . surges thickly and excitedly under the arch of the bridge.
A vast, solid crowd surrounds
. . . the tent containing the body of Vakulinchuk. (*Still on
page 60*) A woman turns to the crowd :
' *Let us not forget him!* '
. . . and she points to the corpse of Vakulinchuk.
The inscription on a sheet of paper : ' *On account of a spoon-
ful of borshch.*'
Angrily, the woman says :
' *On account of a spoonful of borshch.*'
A young man in a sailor's sweater agitatedly reads an address
to the crowd :
' *People of Odessa! Before us lies the body of the brutally
murdered sailor, Grigory Vakulinchuk — murdered by a
senior officer of the squadron battleship, " Prince Tavrich-
esky." Let us have our revenge on the bloodthirsty vampires!
Death to the oppressors! Signed by the crew of the squadron
battleship, " Prince Tavrichesky ".*'
The people listen to him avidly.
Women standing near the tent weep.
An old woman kneels by the corpse of Vakulinchuk and
kisses his hand.
The body of Vakulinchuk with the lighted candle in his
hands.
The old woman weeps.
An old man in pince-nez looks grievously
. . . at the murdered Vakulinchuk. Two old women kneel by
the corpse.
A supercilious-looking man smokes unconcernedly, and looks
on with a smirk

. . . when a woman falls to the ground in grief.

A LASTING MONUMENT TO THE FALLEN WAR-RIORS . . . !

Women begin to sing.

ALL FOR ONE . . .

The whole crowd begins to sing. (*Still on page 60*)

ONE . . .

The dead Vakulinchuk with the lighted candle in his hands.

. . . FOR ALL . . .

A vast crowd around the tent.
Two blind women singing.
A woman weeping.
The whole crowd
. . . with heads bent in woe.
Tears form in the eyes of a dock-worker.
A man nervously touches his forage-cap.
The dock-worker weeps, covering his face with his hand.
The student delivers his speech.
' *Down with the butchers!* '
The crowd
. . . is agitated.
A fist is clenched in hatred.
The crowd
. . . listens to the speaker.
A clenched fist.
The excitement of the crowd grows.
One of the women begins to make a speech.
Again, a fist is clenched in hatred.
The woman turns to the crowd.
An old woman shouts in excitement.
A fist is raised threateningly.

66

Everybody excitedly waves his hands and shouts:
' *Down with the autocrats!* '
The excitement of the crowd
. . . rises
. . . ever higher
. . . and higher,
. . . and draws near
. . . to its peak.
A suspicious-looking man in a straw hat, his hands tucked insolently into his waistcoat, looks on with a disdainful smile.
The woman shouts:
' *Mothers and brothers! Let there be no distinctions or enmities among ourselves!* '
. . . and she exhorts the crowd.
The suspicious-looking man in the straw hat smiles disdainfully.
The woman continues her speech.
The suspicious-looking man in the straw hat cries out:
' *Down with the Jews!* '
. . . and smiles insolently.
The men standing near him
. . . sharply
. . . and angrily,
. . . one
. . . after another,
. . . turn their heads.
The reactionary* continues to smile insolently.
One of the men advances towards him angrily.
The reactionary grows frightened.
The man continues to advance towards him.
The reactionary pulls his straw hat over his eyes and tries to walk away, but he is stopped.

_____

* ' *Chyornosotyenyets* ' in the Russian text: ' a member of the Black Hundred ', a virulent anti-Jewish society.

The man looks at him in fury.
The reactionary
. . . is surrounded by men.
They pull his straw hat over his face and
. . . begin
. . . to attack him.
Pathetically, the student delivers his speech.
The sea of people
. . . surges in agitation.
Pathetically, the student delivers his speech.
The women frenziedly wave their arms.
Pathetically, the student continues his speech.
The women shout in their frenzy.
The student appeals to the crowd :
' *Shoulder to shoulder!* '
The multitude descends the long, narrow steps by the bridge.

THE LAND IS OURS . . . !

Under the arch of the bridge the sea of moving people sways
convulsively.

THE FUTURE IS OURS . . . !

Along the bridge the people move.
The women in the crowd near the tent containing the body
of Vakulinchuk continue to shout in their frenzy.
The sea of people surges with excitement.
Pathetically, the student continues his speech.
The excitement of the crowd
. . . reaches
. . . its peak.

The sailors make their appearance
. . . on the decks and by the gun-turret of the battleship,
. . . and begin to listen to the speakers.

THE DELEGATE FROM THE SHORE . . .

A worker speaks to the sailors :
' *We must inflict a decisive blow on the enemy!* '
He appeals to the sailors :
' *Together with the revolutionary workers throughout all Russia . . .*',
. . . and he exhorts them passionately.
The sailors answer him :
' *We will be victorious!* '
The worker's speech seizes the imagination of the sailors on the decks and
. . . in the watch-tower.
The sailors, taking off their caps,
. . . rapturously
. . . applaud
. . . the delegate.
The sailors standing in the watch-tower also take off their caps and wave their arms to the delegate.

TENSELY AND VIGILANTLY, THE SHORE KEEPS ITS EYE ON THE ' POTEMKIN ' . . .

The inhabitants of the town, standing on the harbour steps, gaze at the battleship in the distance.
On the battleship, the sailors, their heads thrown high,
. . . watch tensely,
. . . as the red flag is raised.
The inhabitants of the town joyfully praise the insurgent battleship. (*Still on page 77*)
The red flag is raised victoriously up the mast of the battleship.

PART FOUR: THE ODESSA STEPS

*IN THOSE MEMORABLE DAYS THE TOWN LIVED
AT ONE WITH THE REBELLIOUS BATTLESHIP . . .*

In the harbour, the townspeople load their sailing-boats with
provisions.

*A FLEET OF WHITE-SAILED YAWLS RACES
THROUGH THE WATER TO THE SIDES OF THE
BATTLESHIP . . .*

The sails of the boats are put up,
. . . and they fill with wind.
The boats push off,
. . . and sail past the town,
. . . and the wharf,
. . . and out into the open sea.
The passing boats are seen as a background to a curved colon-
nade overlooking the water from the height of the town.
A demonstration takes place beneath the arch of the bridge.
In the distance can be seen the white sails of the boats.
On the wharf, an educated young woman, an umbrella in her
hand, and a man — apparently a professor — look ardently,
but with reserve, in the direction of the rebellious battleship.
A group of workers (two men and a woman) tumultuously hail
the rebellious sailors.
The young woman with the umbrella opens it out joyfully
and waves her black-gloved hand, and the man with the
appearance of a professor takes off his hat.
Standing with a young schoolgirl, an elderly woman in pince-
nez rapturously waves her hand.
A student shouts joyfully.
A yacht sails across the sea,

. . . and the fleet of white-sailed yawls.

On the mast of the battleship the red flag flutters victoriously.

The boats sail towards the battleship.

The sailors on board the battleship wave their caps in delight.

The boats

. . . sail up,

. . . one after another,

. . . to the sides of the battleship. (*Still on page 77*)

Sailors pull the oars of the rowing-boats.

The sailors on board the battleship wave their caps in delight.

The sailing-boats draw up by the side of the battleship.

Sailors from the battleship quickly descend the gangway.

Sailing-boats and rowing-boats draw up.

The sailing-boats

. . . drop their sails.

The sailors on board the battleship wave their caps in delight.

Sailing-boats

. . . surround the battleship.

The sailors on board the battleship wave their caps in delight.

The inhabitants of the town, standing on the harbour steps, look at the battleship in the distance.

A woman with a live goose in her hands climbs up the gangway and gives it to the sailors.

On the sailing-boats, bread is passed from hand to hand.

The inhabitants of the town, standing on the harbour steps, look at the battleship in the distance.

The people in the sailing-boats look at the sailors on board the battleship.

Cigarettes, a sucking-pig are passed to the sailors,

. . . a crateful of poultry,

. . . geese.

On board the battleship, the inhabitants of the town embrace the sailors.

Along the gangway are carried a basket of eggs,

. . . another sucking-pig.

The inhabitants of the town, standing on the harbour steps,
. . . look into the distance,
. . . and hail the battleship.
A lady with a veil and lorgnette
. . . and a lady in an expensive white dress, an umbrella over
her arm, also look at the battleship. Past them, a legless
invalid drags himself on his hands.
The lady in the expensive white dress, an umbrella over her
arm, waves elegantly in the direction of the rebellious battleship.
From behind the lady with the veil and lorgnette, the legless
invalid moves on his hands,
. . . and he looks in the direction of the battleship.
The lady with the veil looks through her lorgnette at the rebellious battleship.
The legless invalid joyfully waves his cap with one hand.
A woman draped with a shawl stands beside her small son.
On the mast of the battleship the red flag flutters victoriously.
The woman, draped with a shawl, and her son look joyfully
at the battleship.
A girl and a boy wave their small hands in delight.
The crowd, standing on the harbour steps, tumultuously hails
the insurgent battleship.

SUDDENLY . . .

A woman with bobbed hair throws back her head in terror.
The crowd on the steps shudders and begins to run down the
steps.
The legless invalid, trying to save himself, leaps precipitatley
on his hands down one of the high balustrades flanking the
steps.
A rank of soldiers draws near to the top of the long, broad
steps.
The lady with the veil and lorgnette, having fallen, raises
herself and runs down the steps.

73

In terror the crowd runs down the steps.

Fatally wounded, a man begins to fall.

In the instant before his death, the steps appear fleetingly in front of his eyes. He falls

. . . onto the steps.

A small boy, wounded, falls nearby.

In terror the crowd runs down the steps.

The boy clutches his head with his hands.

In terror the crowd runs down the steps.

Relentless, like a machine, ranks of soldiers with rifles trailed descend the steps.

In terror the crowd runs down the steps.

Behind the balustrade a group of terrified women hide — among them the elderly woman in pince-nez.

Men leap from the balustrade onto the ground.

Behind one of the balustrades a man and a woman hide.

Behind the other balustrade an old man in pince-nez, a small schoolboy and a woman hide. The old man in pince-nez is unexpectedly hit by a bullet.

A rank of soldiers fires into the crowd.

The man hidden with the woman behind one of the balustrades falls dead.

In terror the crowd runs down the steps.

A man jumps over the wounded old man in pince-nez. The old man raises himself and looks at him.

In terror the crowd runs down the steps.

The old man in pince-nez looks from behind the balustrade.

The woman draped with a shawl runs down the steps, holding her small son by the hand.

The ranks of soldiers aim, and fire into the crowd.

The son of the woman draped with a shawl falls onto the steps. (*Still on page 78*)

Mechanically, the woman draped with a shawl continues to run down the steps.

The fallen boy raises himself and shouts.

The fleeing mother stops
... and turns.
The boy falls back, unconscious.
In horror the mother tears at her hair.
In terror the crowd runs down the steps — over the fallen boy.
Her eyes crazed, the mother goes up the steps.
In terror the crowd runs down the steps.
... trampling the slaughtered boy.
In terror the crowd runs down the steps.
The fleeing people
... trample the slaughtered boy.
Her eyes crazed, the mother goes up the steps.
The crowd runs down the steps.
Her hands to her head in horror, the mother goes up the steps.
The crowd tramples the slaughtered boy.
Her hands to her head in horror, the mother goes up the steps.
The crowd runs down the steps.
Her slaughtered son in her arms, the mother goes up the steps
... towards a rank of soldiers.
In terror the crowd runs down the steps.
The elderly woman in pince-nez, hidden behind the balustrade, exhorts
... the women with her
... to advance towards the soldiers, in order to stop the massacre.
Her slaughtered son in her arms, the demented mother goes up the steps. (*Still on page 78*)
In a frenzy, the elderly woman in pince-nez exhorts the women with her.
' *Come! Let us plead with them!* '
She regards them boldly.
In terror the crowd continues to run down the steps.
The elderly woman in pince-nez smiles
... encouragingly

. . . at the women with her and at the old men,
. . . all frozen with fear.

Relentless, like a machine, the rank of soldiers with rifles trailed descends the steps.

Her slaughtered son in her arms, the demented mother goes up the steps.

The women are frozen with fear.

The elderly woman in pince-nez smiles encouragingly.

A young girl,
. . . the old men,
. . . men, an old woman,
. . . and an invalid on crutches
. . . stand up behind her.

The rank of soldiers fires into the crowd.

In terror the crowd continues to run down the steps.

Her slaughtered son in her arms, the demented mother goes up the steps.

Led by the elderly woman in pince-nez, the group of women and old men go up the steps towards the rank of soldiers,
. . . and pleadingly hold out their hands to them.

Through the corpses strewn on the steps, her slaughtered son in her arms, the mother continues to go up the steps.

Through the corpses strewn on the steps, relentless, the rank of soldiers with rifles trailed continues to descend the steps.

Her slaughtered son in her arms, going up the steps strewn with corpses, the mother shouts to the soldiers : (*Still on page 79*) ' *Hear me! Don't shoot!* '

Inexorably, the rank of soldiers moves on.

The shadows of the soldiers fall on the steps.

Her slaughtered son in her arms, the mother shouts again to the soldiers : (*Still on page 80*)
' *My boy is badly hurt!* '

She draws close to the rank of soldiers, their rifles aimed
. . . and to the officer, his sabre raised.

Led by the elderly woman in pince-nez, the group of women

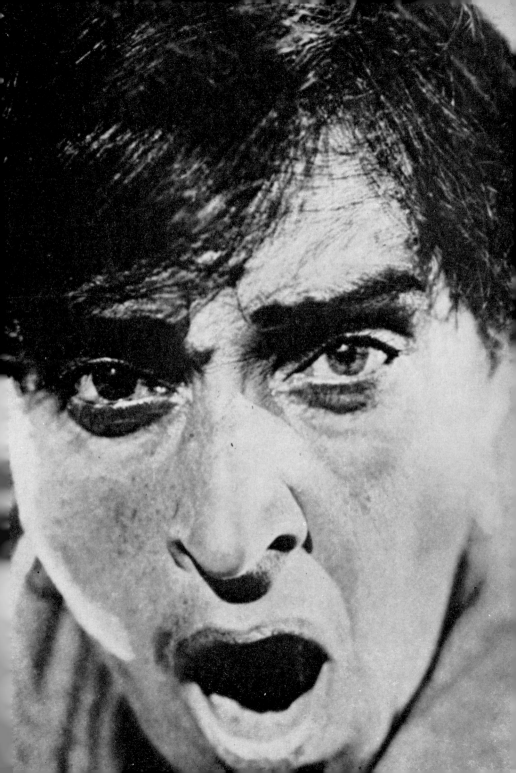

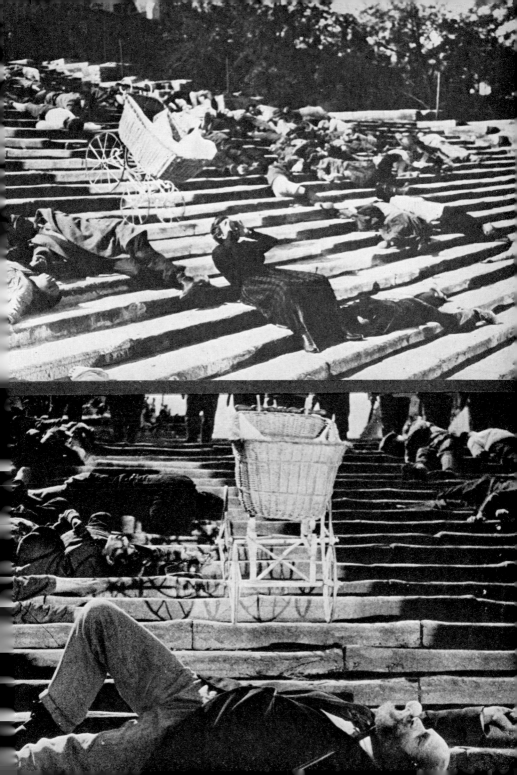

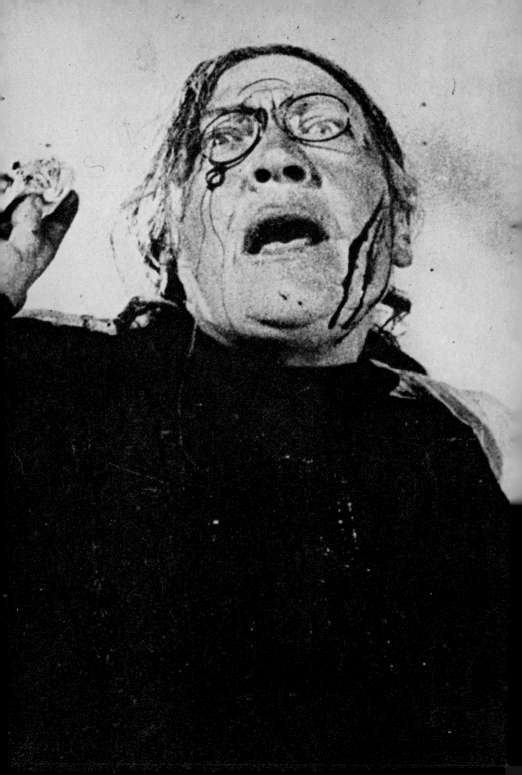

and old men,
. . . pleading,
. . . go up the steps.
The officer lowers his sabre, and a volley is fired.
Her slaughtered son in her arms, the mother falls onto the steps.
At the bottom of the steps, the people run onto the carriage-way,
. . . and horsemen charge them.
Her slaughtered son held tight to her breast, the mother lies on her back.
Her hands are arranged in the form of a cross, and
. . . over them creep the advancing shadows of the soldiers.

THE COSSACKS . . .

The cossacks charge straight at the crowd, and
. . . the people are trampled by the horses' hooves and beaten with the whips of the horsemen.
A rank of soldiers descends the steps (*Still on page 80*)
. . . and fires into the crowd.
The group of women and old men, pressing themselves against the balustrade, go up the steps.
The rank of soldiers fires volley after volley into the crowd.
The group of women and old men fall onto the steps.
The legs of the soldiers move on. (*Stills on page 81*)
A beautiful woman shields a pram containing a child from the fleeing people.
Relentless, like a machine, the rank of soldiers descends the steps.
The beautiful woman opens her mouth in terror
. . . and clings to the side of the pram.
With her body, she shields the child in the pram from the fleeing people. (*Still on page 82*)
The rank of soldiers descends the steps
. . . and fires.

85

In terrible pain, the young mother throws back her head.
The pram with the child comes to rest at the edge of the steps.
The young mother, her mouth open in terror,
. . . clutches her dress with her hands.
The fleeing people are trampled by the horses' hooves and beaten with the whips of the cossacks.
Blood on the young mother's stomach.
The young mother, her mouth open,
. . . begins to fall,
. . . and the pram with the child rolls to the very edge of the steps.
The rank of soldiers with rifles trailed
. . . descends the steps.
The young mother, falling onto the steps,
. . . pushes
. . . the pram with the child.
A cossack attacks a man with his whip.
The fleeing people are trampled by the horses' hooves and beaten with the whips of the cossacks.
Fallen, the young mother
. . . jolts
. . . the pram with the child
. . . over the edge of the steps.
The elderly woman in pince-nez is frozen with horror.
The pram with the child
. . . bounces
. . . down the steps. (*Still on page 83*)
The young mother lies dead on the steps.
On the carriage-way, the cossacks beat the crowd with whips, and,
. . . at the foot of the steps,
. . . a rank of soldiers fires point-blank at the people.
The pram with the child bounces over the steps.
The elderly woman in pince-nez is frozen with horror.

The pram with the child bounces over the steps.

A terrified student presses himself into the corner of a building.

At the foot of the steps, the rank of soldiers fires volley after volley into the crowd.

The pram with the child leaps across the steps.

A terrified student presses himself into the corner of a building.

Down the steps,

... over the corpses,

... careers the pram with the child. (*Still on page 83*)

The rank of soldiers fires into the crowd.

The pram with the child careers over the corpses down the steps.

The student pressed into the corner of the building shouts in terror.

The pram with the child overturns.

A cossack brandishes

... his sword,

... and puts out an eye of the elderly woman in pince-nez. (*Still on page 84*)

The battleship : the gun-turret looms ominously.

AND THEN THE CANNONS OF THE BATTLESHIP OPEN FIRE IN RETALIATION AGAINST THE SAVAGERY OF THE ARMED FORCES OF ODESSA . . .

The muzzles of the cannons, pointed menacingly towards the town.

THE BULL'S EYE — THE ODESSA THEATRE . . . !

The sculpture on the pediment of the theatre.

THE ODESSA THEATRE — THE TOWN'S MILITARY HEADQUARTERS . . .

The cannons of the battleship open fire (*Stills on page 101*)
.. at the cupids

. . . adorning
. . . the cornice of the theatre.
A shell bursts
. . . against the iron gates of the theatre building,
. . . enshrouding everything in smoke.
The sculptures : a lion dormant,
. . . a lion with evil face raised,
. . . a lion up on its paws, snarling.
The iron gates of the theatre building
. . . are enshrouded in smoke.
The smoke disperses — to reveal that the theatre building has
been destroyed.

PART FIVE: MEETING THE SQUADRON

*ON THE BATTLESHIP, MEETINGS CONTINUE PAS-
SIONATELY UNTIL EVENING . . .*

A speaker cries to the sailors:
'*The people of Odessa look to you for their liberation. Dis-
embark now, and the army will join forces with you.*'
The speaker
. . . continues. The muzzles of the cannons loom menacingly.
The sailors
. . . argue among themselves.
One of the sailors says:
'*We cannot disembark. The admiralty squadron has begun
to move against us.*'
He continues to speak.
The sailors wave their arms about excitedly.
The sailor exhorts his comrades,
. . . who wave to him
. . . with their caps.
The sailor exhorts his comrades.
The sailors wave their arms about excitedly.
The sailor passionately exhorts his comrades.
One of the sailors listening to him is lost in thought.
The sailor continues to exhort his comrades,
. . . but the other sailor interrupts him.

*WITH ONE HEART THEY DECIDE TO FACE THE
SQUADRON . . .*

The empty deck.

A NIGHT OF ANXIETY BEGINS . . .

The flag comes down.

The moon appears from behind the clouds
Moonlight plays upon the water.
On the battleship, the watch looks tensely into the distance.
The sea splashes gently.
The watch moves along the side of the battleship.
The sea splashes gently.
A sailor gazes tensely into the distance.
The silhouette of the battleship stands out starkly and majestic-
ally in the moonlight.
The motionless needles
. . . of the pressure-gauges.
By the engines — sleeping sailors.
The watch looks tensely into the darkness.
A searchlight directed on the water.
The watch and the sailor gaze into the darkness.
The searchlight directed on the water.
By the engines — sleeping sailors.
The motionless needles of the pressure-gauges.

THE SQUADRON CREEPS UP IN THE DARKNESS . . .

Murk over the water.
The squadron on the horizon.
Murk over the water.
Matyushenko, fighting against sleep,
. . . smokes
. . . in one of the cabins.
Smoke pours from the funnels of a passing ship. (*Still on page
102*)
By the engines — sleeping sailors.
The helmsman asleep at the wheel.
By the engines — sleeping sailors.
The searchlight directed on the water.
In a cabin, a sailor asleep on a divan.
Matyushenko, with other sailors, awakens the helmsman.
The cabin : the sailor asleep on the divan.

Another sailor at the wheel.

THROATS HOARSE FROM CONTINUAL SPEECH
BREATHE HARSHLY AND UNEVENLY . . .

The cabin : sailors asleep
. . . on the divan,
. . . in a deck-chair.
Matyushenko enters the cabin and looks at the sleeping sailors.
The sailor on the divan awakens.
Sailors close the shutter over the searchlight.
Matyushenko talks with the awakened sailor,
. . . and goes out of the cabin.
The sailor turns over onto his other side.
Sailors close the shutter over the searchlight.
The sailor on the divan sleeps.
Sailors run over to a handrail.
By the engines — the sailors roll over uneasily in their sleep.
The sailor on the divan awakens again.
The helmsman at the wheel.
A sailor by the handrail beckons to another.
By the engines — the sailors roll over uneasily in their sleep.
The sailor by the handrail
. . . looks through a telescope.
The sailors by the handrail gaze tensely into the distance.
The motionless needles
. . . of the pressure-gauges.
Sailors look through a pair of binoculars
. . . and the telescope.
The watch looks through the binoculars.
The pressure-gauges.
Sailors look through the binoculars and the telescope.
The watch looks through the binoculars.
A sailor in the watch-tower shouts.
The sailor turns the telescope.
Near the muzzle of a cannon, a sailor gazes into the darkness.

The watches look into the distance.
The sailor turns the telescope.
The squadron is visible on the horizon.
The sailor looking through the telescope bends and cries :
' *Squadron on the horizon!* '
The sailor near the muzzle of the cannon turns quickly towards the cry.
The sailor again looks through the telescope.
The alarmed figures
. . . of the sailors.
Matyushenko rapidly descends the ladder to the cabin.
In an instant, the sailor in the deck-chair is awake,
. . . and the sailor on the divan.
The one
. . . and the other raise themselves,
. . . jerkily
. . . stand up,
. . . and quickly run out.
A running sailor can be seen through a grating.
The sailors run up to Matyushenko and question him.
In the cabin, Matyushenko stops a young sailor.
The young sailor looks confusedly at Matyushenko.
Matyushenko throws off his jacket.
The young sailor tightens the jacket round himself, and Matyushenko takes the midshipman's cap off the young sailor's head.
Sailors climbing up holdfasts.
Matyushenko puts a sailor's cap on the young sailor's head.
The young sailor ascends the ladder from the cabin, followed by Matyushenko.
The sailors rush up the holdfasts,
. . . up the deck ladder,
. . . up to a platform by the funnel.
The sailors on the platform can see
. . . the squadron on the horizon.

They continue to look at the squadron on the horizon.
The sailor looks through the telescope.
Sailors looking into the distance,
. . . climbing up the holdfasts,
. . . ascending to the platform by the funnel,
. . . on the platform.
Matyushenko blows on his pipe.

ALL HANDS ON DECK . . . !

The bugler
. . . sounds his call.
A sailor blows on his pipe.
The sailors come running.

ACTION STATIONS . . . !

The bugler
. . . sounds his call.
About the deck
. . . the sailors run.
Sailors remove the tarpaulins from the cannons.
In the gun-turret, a gunner
. . . prepares
. . . for battle.
About the deck the sailors run.
Matyushenko blows on his pipe.
About the deck the sailors run.
Sailors run
. . . to the engine-room.
The helmsman and Matyushenko speak over the telephone
. . . to the engineer in the engine-room.
Matyushenko speaks over the telephone
. . . to the engineer.
About the deck the sailors run.
Sailors move
. . . the heavy shells

. . . up the lift to the cannons.

The sailors remove the tarpaulins from the cannons.

The engineer, speaking on the telephone, passes an order to a comrade.

The engineer pulls a lever.

The telephones ring in the engine-room.

Sailors descend the gangway and pull up the handrail.

The engineer pulls a lever.

The sailors

. . . raise

. . . the gangway.

The engineer pulls a lever.

The sailors

. . . suspend

. . . the gangway

. . . along the side of the battleship.

A tarpaulin is spread over the deck.

Sailors take the heavy shells from the lift,

. . . and lay them on the tarpaulin,

. . . one

. . . after another.

Matyushenko stands by the helm and shouts into the speaking-tube.

FULL SPEED AHEAD . . .

The engineer listens on the telephone.

Behind the helmsman, Matyushenko speaks on the telephone.

The sailors

. . . working in the engine-room.

Smoke pouring from the funnels.

The engineer presses a lever.

Faster and faster

. . . the engines run.

The battleship carves its way through the sea, dividing the water into tall waves.

94

The calm sea splashes gently against the shore.
The battleship carves its way through the sea, dividing the water into tall waves.
Ever faster and faster
. . . the engines run.
The battleship carves its way through the sea, dividing the water into tall waves.
At full speed,
. . . the engines run.
Smoke pours from the funnels.
Behind it, the battleship leaves a shining wake and clouds of smoke.

Matyushenko, speaking on the telephone, receives a message from a sailor approaching at the run, and he gives the order to the helmsman to turn the wheel.
The gun-turrets swing menacingly.
The gunner is prepared for battle.
The muzzles of the cannons are raised menacingly.
The gunner looks at his sights.
The muzzles of the cannons are raised.
The gunner looks at his sights.
The prow of the battleship cuts through the water,
. . . raising great waves on all sides.
Standing by the helm, Matyushenko looks through a telescope.
The squadron is visible on the horizon.
Matyushenko speaks to the helmsman.
The needle of a pressure-gauge jumps about — and moves up.
The engineer speaks on the telephone.
The needle jumps about — and moves higher.
The gunner is prepared for battle.
The squadron on the horizon.
The engines at full speed.
The gunner by his sights.
The gunner swings
. . . his cannon.

The engines at full speed.
The needle of the pressure-gauge jumps about.

MAXIMUM SPEED . . . !

The needle as high as it can go.
The engines at maximum speed.
Great waves caused by the passage of the battleship.
The water bubbles and foams.
Smoke pours from the funnels.
The helmsman, turning the wheel, listens to Matyushenko.
Visible in the distance — the squadron.

THE 'POTEMKIN' AND DESTROYER NO. 267 . . .

Alongside the battleship — a destroyer.
Standing by the helm, Matyushenko looks into the distance.

THE SQUADRON ADVANCES . . .

The squadron draws ever nearer and nearer.
Smoke pours from the funnels.
Great waves caused by the passage of the battleship.
The water bubbles and foams.
Matyushenko, standing by the helm, gives a signal.
The gun-turret swings menacingly.

THE SQUADRON DRAWS NEAR . . . !

Ever nearer and nearer
. . . draws the squadron.
The gunner sights his cannon.
The gun-turret swings menacingly.
Sailors carrying a shell.
The muzzles of the cannons loom menacingly.
Smoke pours from the funnels.
Behind it, the battleship leaves a shining wake and clouds of smoke.
Standing by the helm, Matyushenko looks into the distance.

The squadron draws nearer.
Matyushenko is plunged in thought.
His hand goes to the speaking-tube.
' Give the signal: " Join us " ! '
He replaces the speaking-tube.
A sailor signals with flags,
. . . and another looks through a telescope.
' Join . . .'
On ropes, the flags go up the mast.
'. . . us! '
On ropes,
. . . the flags
. . . go up
. . . the mast.
The battleship raises great waves
. . . on all sides.
The squadron draws ever nearer and nearer.
Smoke pours
. . . from the funnels of an approaching ship.
The muzzle of a cannon aimed towards the enemy.
The helmsman looks through a telescope.
The gunners await the signal.

THE ENEMY WITHIN RANGE . . .

The helmsman looks through a telescope.
The gunners
. . . await the signal.
A sailor with a shell in his arms.
Sailors with shells in their arms.

ALL FOR ONE . . .

The cannons of the enemy turn slowly,
. . . point towards the *Potemkin,*
. . . are menacingly
. . . raised.

ONE FOR ALL . . .

On the mast of the battleship the red flag flutters victoriously.
Alongside the battleship — the destroyer.
A cannon raised
. . . looms menacingly.
Standing by the helm, Matyushenko looks into the distance.
The enemy squadron is near.
The gunners embrace each other before battle.
A cannon is raised,
. . . and looms menacingly.
The gunners await the signal.
The cannon looms menacingly.
Standing by the helm, Matyushenko shouts.
The muzzles of all the cannons of the battleship
. . . are directed
. . . menacingly
. . . towards the enemy.

TO FIRE . . .

The gunners tensely await the signal.
Matyushenko looks uneasily into the distance.
He blows on his pipe.
A cannon looms menacingly.

OR NOT . . .

A gunner tensely awaits the signal.
The engines running.
The imperial eagle on the prow of the battleship.
Sailors with shells in their arms, tensely expectant.
Shells on the tarpaulin.
The gunner motionless.
Suddenly, a smile appears on the face of one of the sailors.
' Brothers! '
Joyfully,
. . . the sailors

. . . break out into laughter.
The sailors run out onto the prow of the battleship.
The sailors are overcome
. . . with joy.
On the mast of the battleship the red flag flutters victoriously.
The muzzles of the cannons are lowered.
The sailors on board the battleship tumultuously wave their caps. (*Still on page 102*)
In return,
. . . from the sides of the ships of the squadron passing,
. . . the sailors joyfully
. . . wave their caps.

WITHIN THE HEARING OF THE TSARIST ADMIRALS, BROTHERLY CHEERS SOUND ACROSS THE WATER . . .

From the sides of the ships of the squadron passing,
. . . the sailors
. . . joyfully wave their caps.
Without a shot being fired, a ship of the admiralty squadron goes past the rebellious battleship.

AND WITH THE RED FLAG OF FREEDOM PROUDLY FLUTTERING, WITHOUT A SINGLE SHOT BEING FIRED, THE INSURGENT BATTLESHIP PASSES THROUGH THE RANKS OF THE SQUADRON . . .

The sailors on the decks of the battleship,
. . . on the mast and in the watch-tower
. . . tumultuously wave their caps in the air. (*Still on page 103*)
Victoriously, the insurgent battleship passes through the ranks of the squadron.
Joyfully, the sailors on the mast, in the watch-tower,
. . . on the decks
. . . and on the prow of the battleship
. . . wave their caps in the air.

Great waves caused by the passage of the battleship.
The tall prow of the rebellious battleship moves victoriously
onwards. (*Still on page 104*)

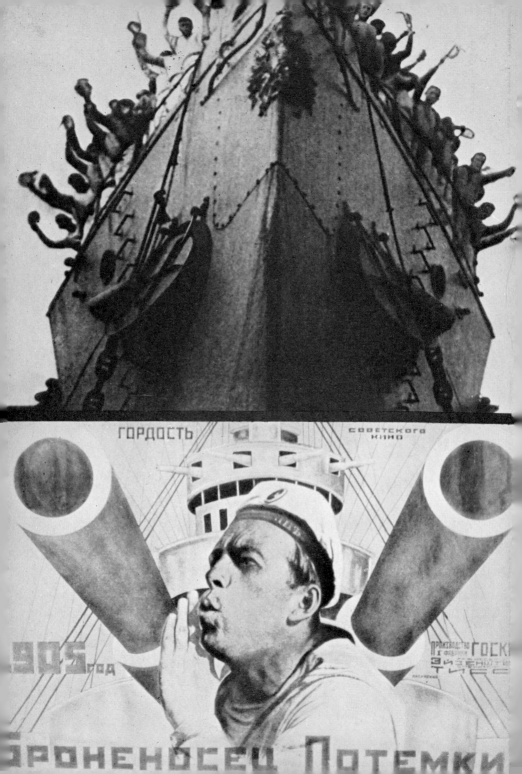

ГОРДОСТЬ СОВЕТСКОГО КИНО

905 год

ПРОИЗВОДСТВО 1 фабрики ГОСКИНО

БРОНЕНОСЕЦ ПОТЕМКИ